Christmas

PROGRAMS, DRAMAS, AND SKITS

Carpenter's Son Publishing

Christmas Programs, Dramas, and Skits

©2016 by Paul Shepherd

Published by Carpenter's Son Publishing, Franklin, Tennessee.

Published in association with Larry Carpenter of Christian Book Services, LLC. www.christianbookservices.com

Scripture is used from the New King James Version, © 1982 by Thomas Nelson, Inc. All rights reserved. Used by permission.

Edited by Alice Sullivan and Gail Fallen

Cover and Interior Layout Design by Suzanne Lawing

Printed in the United States of America

978-1-942587-52-1

Contents

Kids

Youth

Adults

Kids

The Pirate Who Tried to Steal Christmas

Written through inspiration of the Holy Spirit
by Dianne Garvis © 2007

SUMMARY: *A tough pirate plans to steal the joy of those worshiping baby Jesus but finds his missing happiness and the true meaning of Christmas.*

CHARACTERS:
Narrator
Choir
Captain Blythe, a pirate captain
Snively, the first mate
3 or 4 pirate crew members who can double as church members
Little Girl with curly hair

SETTING: *pirate ship; church sanctuary*

PROPS: *nativity scene*

COSTUMES: *choir robes, pirate costumes (with contemporary clothing underneath for the crew members), pirate captain's hat, contemporary winter clothing for the little girl*

NARRATOR: 'Twas the night before Christmas, when all through the house, not a creature was stirring, not even a mouse.

Pirate music plays.

Choir enters—stomping in—singing pirate song.

NARRATOR: But this story starts upon the high sea; the pirates were restless due to the Captain's decree.

CAPTAIN BLYTHE: There'll be no more Christmas! No more holiday cheer! We'll pillage their toys. Their best Christmas was . . . LAST YEAR! Replace treasures with crossbones; leave skulls on their beds! No more visions of sugarplums will dance in their heads.

NARRATOR: The Captain summoned his first mate with a billowing shout! Snively came tottering, squeaking his words out.

SNIVELY: You called for me, Captain? What can I do?

CAPTAIN BLYTHE: Snively, it's time to gather me crew!

SNIVELY: Ye-e-es, sir! Captain, you brilliant buccaneer, I'll gather the men and bring them right here.

NARRATOR: So off he did scurry, Captain Blythe he must please. When he got to the deck, the crew was scrubbing on their knees.

SNIVELY: Oh d-d-dear! Your cleaning is through. Captain Blythe said it's time to sail the Briny Blue.

NARRATOR: As they got to the bow, the sails began to quiver. The commands of this marauder would cause a rogue to shiver.

CAPTAIN BLYTHE: Cast off, you mangy dogs! Hoist anchor! Set sail! Another notch in me scabbard to hear sad children wail!

NARRATOR: Then from the top deck the crew heard him call,

CAPTAIN BLYTHE: Now cast away, cast away, cast away all!

Music track fades in slowly.

NARRATOR: Back on the mainland, families gathered in prayer. A celebration of Christmas, without even a care.

Choir sings medley of Christmas carols.

NARRATOR: At that precise moment, Captain Blythe did appear. It seems their genuine joy had brought him to tears. He was watching them worship, their Savior, the King, perplexed for he thought they'd been greedy for things. This black-hearted scoundrel suddenly felt his heart ache, for he'd wasted his life; it was too much to take.

CAPTAIN BLYTHE: Arrrgh! Blast! I've been a babbling fool. I should walk the plank, for I've been so cruel.

NARRATOR: Then from across the room there came the smallest wee girl. Her face like an angel; her hair worn in curls.

LITTLE GIRL: What's wrong, Mister Pirate? Please, sir. Don't cry.

NARRATOR: As she dried off his tears, she looked into his eye.

LITTLE GIRL: You see that little baby? Jesus is His name. To save us from death is the reason He came. He loves you, nice man, so please don't be sad. No one has ever been unforgivably bad.

NARRATOR: Captain spoke not a word. Sinking straight to his knees, overcome with repentance, he cried . . .

CAPTAIN BLYTHE: Father, forgive me. PLEASE!

NARRATOR: Then he sprang to his feet, feeling light as a feather.

He begins to dance around, exclaiming,

CAPTAIN BLYTHE: I feel SO MUCH BETTER!

NARRATOR: The town heard him proclaim as he sailed out of sight . . .

CAPTAIN BLYTHE: Merry Christmas to ALL! And to ALL a blessed night!

Sound track begins—final triumphant Christmas song.

Uprooted

by Diana C. Derringer © 2015

SUMMARY: *A Christmas tree relives the trauma and revelation of its Christmas experience.*

CHARACTER: *Christmas Tree*

SETTING: *a family room*

PROPS: *wrapped gifts, nativity scene*

COSTUME: *green clothing, such as a stiff A-line dress; brown socks, or tights and shoes*

The Christmas Tree, surrounded by gifts and with a nativity scene in front, speaks with agony.

CHRISTMAS TREE: How horrible! How absolutely horrible . . . the day the humans came, all bundled in their warm clothing, laughing and singing, with *(shudder)* those shovels over their shoulders. They walked through us, looking us over, discussing our shape and height like we weren't even there. And then they stopped right in front of me. *(shrink back)* Nodding their heads and saying I looked perfect, I began to relax . . . until the shoveling began. *(higher voice pitch)* Around and around and around they went with those shovels, digging deeper and deeper until they uncovered all my roots. *(shudder)* Then they pulled me completely out of the ground! I thought I was going to die!

They bundled my roots in a rough brown cloth and tied it around my trunk. I appreciated the warmth, but that didn't last long. They began dragging me away from the only home I'd ever known, laughing like they couldn't care less. Then they threw me on top of their car and tied me down on that hard metal top, and the agony only grew worse. As they drove away, the wind and snow beat on my branches. *(Sway from side to side.)* I thought they would never stop, but finally they pulled into a driveway. More humans came running out of the house to pull me off the car. Close behind them came two dogs and a cat determined to rip me to shreds.

Why? Why was this happening?

After the miserable cold, they took me inside the house to a room with a roaring fireplace. Whew! *(wipe brow)* Talk about a change! They spent a few more minutes admiring my beauty, *(adjust hair)* such as it was after that awful ride. Then they dumped my roots in a bucket—a bucket, for heaven's sake! No mountaintop, no sunrise or sunset, no other trees . . . There I stood: in a house in a cold metal bucket. *(pause)* I have to admit the dirt and water did provide some much-needed refreshment. I slurped that water faster than they could pour.

Then, yikes, what did they do next? They covered me in strands of little lights. Now, if that won't suck the moisture right out of your branches, I don't know what will. But they were just getting started. Next came box after box of glittery, sparkly, funny-looking objects, and they hung every single one on me. I wasn't a tree any longer. I was a billboard!

But slowly the mood changed. *(reverently, gesturing toward nativity beneath)* Underneath my branches, they placed what looked like a little barn. Inside they arranged a few animals, a couple of humans, and then a baby in a feeding trough! Why would they place a baby in a feeding trough? *(pause)* Anyway, near the trough they placed more humans on their knees with their heads bowed.

As they talked about the meaning of all this, I listened carefully, and what an amazing story. They said that baby came to save the world. He gave up the splendor of heaven in order to sacrifice His life for others, and He teaches that everyone who follows Him must also die to self.

I wonder . . . I wonder if perhaps the giving of myself might also make a difference.

Lights out.

Michael and the Toy Truck

by Alice Sullivan © 2015

SUMMARY: *Children in Mrs. Fay's classroom learn that Christmas is about the birth of a Savior, not pretty decorations.*

CHARACTERS:
Mrs. Fay, teacher
Children:
Ellie: child with doll
Grayson
Lucy
Zack
Michael: child with the toy truck

DIRECTOR'S NOTE: *Children may be called by their real names, if preferred.*

SETTING: *children's classroom*

PROPS: *Christmas tree, ornaments, box or bucket for ornaments, large toy dump truck (or similar toy with a bed), doll, white paper towels*

All the children (except Michael) are gathered around the tree helping Mrs. Fay hang the ornaments. Michael is playing with his toy truck a few feet away.

MRS. FAY: Ellie, that's a beautiful ornament! Yes, place it right next to the silver bells.

ELLIE: Like this?

MRS. FAY: Perfect! Zack, which one have you picked out?

ZACK: I have a snowman! I'm going to put him high on a limb so he can see everything.

MRS. FAY: Wonderful!

Children continue to select and hang ornaments. Michael scoots in with his toy truck, takes a few ornaments off the tree and places them in the back of his truck, and scoots away again to the side of the room. He continues playing alone. Mrs. Fay notices, but doesn't say anything.

MRS. FAY: Grayson, what's your favorite ornament?

GRAYSON: I like this reindeer! He has a red nose like a clown.

MRS. FAY: That's Rudolph the Red-Nosed Reindeer!

GRAYSON: He looks like my dog, Ollie!

Grayson plays with his ornament a bit and then places it on the tree.

MRS. FAY: That's sweet. Lucy—

Michael scoots over and takes a few more ornaments off the tree, places them in the bed of his toy truck, and scoots away. Mrs. Fay is flustered.

MRS. FAY: Um . . . Lucy, which ornament is your favorite?

LUCY: I like the snowflakes best. Mamma says every one is different, and they're fun to catch on your tongue!

MRS. FAY: That's exactly right! No two snowflakes are alike. Just like people.

Michael comes by a third time to take ornaments, and Mrs. Fay finally says something.

MRS. FAY: Michael, what are you doing? Why are you taking the ornaments off the tree? Don't you want to help decorate for Christmas?

MICHAEL: I am.

MRS. FAY: You are what?

MICHAEL: I am decorating.

MRS. FAY: What are you decorating?

MICHAEL: I'm decorating a bed for baby Jesus.

All children stop and look over at the bed of the truck, filled with ornaments.

ZACK: You can't put a baby in there. He'd fall out!

MICHAEL: No he won't. See? I put all the soft ornaments on the bottom and the bigger ones on the side.

MRS. FAY: Michael, that's so sweet, but why does baby Jesus need a bed?

All children are gathered around the toy truck now. Some are kneeling.

MICHAEL: He's a special baby, the Son of God, and He brings good news to us all.

All characters pause, and lights go out. Offstage, someone reads Luke 2:1–14 aloud. Lights come back on after the reading.

GRAYSON: So, where's the baby?

ELLIE: I have a doll!

Ellie runs to her cubby (or table) and grabs her doll. She places it in the back of the truck, on top of the ornaments.

ZACK: *(makes a face)* This doesn't look right.

MICHAEL: I know what we need!

Michael runs to the side of the room, grabs a roll of paper towels, and returns. Then he wraps the doll in paper towels and places it on the ornaments.

LUCY: That looks cozy!

MRS. FAY: Children, this is just beautiful. Why don't we all sing a Christmas song? What about "Silent Night"?

ALL CHILDREN: Yeah!

Children begin to sing and lights fade out.

Santa Falls Short

by Diana C. Derringer © 2015

SUMMARY: *A child contemplates the shortcomings of Santa when compared to Jesus.*

CHARACTER: *Child*

SETTING: *a child's bedroom*

PROPS: *a ragged stuffed animal*

COSTUME: *contemporary child's clothing*

Child sits on the floor, holding and talking to a stuffed animal.

CHILD: Just think, Rags, only five more days till Christmas! Are you excited? *(Shake animal's head up and down.)* Me too! *(forefinger under chin)* I wonder what Santa will bring this year. Maybe he'll have a new friend for you. Would you like that? *(Shake animal's head up and down.)* What fun we could have! *(Hug animal tightly.)* But nobody will ever take your place. Don't you worry about that.

(Start singing "Santa Claus Is Coming to Town," then stop suddenly.) You know what, Rags? I've been thinking a lot lately, and some things about Santa sorta' bother me. I mean, why does he only show up once a year? If

he loves us and wants to give us good stuff, why wait till Christmas? We might need him other times too. Mommy says Jesus stays with us all the time and never leaves us. I think I like that plan better.

And you know what else? Santa only brings us presents if we're good, and a few times I've not been so sure if I would get anything! Do you know how hard it is for little kids to be good all the time? *(Pause, holding animal out.)* Trust me, it's not easy! But Mommy says Jesus loves us just the way we are, no matter what! That's a relief. Of course, Mommy also says Jesus wants us to be good and will help us be good if we let Him in our lives. I don't know all about that yet, but Mommy says I will when the time is right.

And why does Santa come sneaking down chimneys in the middle of the night when everybody's sleeping? Looks like he would just walk right up to the door in broad daylight and say, *(Raise one arm of stuffed animal.)* "Hi, I'm Santa, and here's your present." Wouldn't that be great? Of course, I can't see Jesus either, but I can talk to Him any time I want to. If I get scared of storms, or I'm playing, or I'm getting ready to eat bananas and peanut butter, or I fall off the swing, or I'm all dressed for bed, I can talk to Jesus and He listens. If I need to watch what I'm doing, I don't even have to close my eyes and bow my head. He listens anyway. Want me to show you? *(Look up, smiling and lifting animal.)* "Hi, Jesus, this is my best friend, Rags." *(Lower head and look at Rags.)* See, wasn't that easy?

Rags, have you noticed how Santa talks? About all he says is, *(lower voice)* "Ho, ho, ho, have you been a good little boy or girl?" That's not much, is it? But there's a whole book just filled with stuff Jesus said. Things like be kind to other people, and He loves us, and He'll help us when we mess up . . . so many good things, I can't even remember them all. How about that?

I guess maybe Santa tries the best he can, but seems to me he could learn some great lessons from Jesus. Probably we all could, huh?

Skip off stage, holding Rags.

Birthday Presents

by Diana C. Derringer © 2015

SUMMARY: *Children learn that they give to Jesus when they give to people in need.*

CHARACTERS:
Ms. Linda, teacher
Children:
Kelsey
Corey
Lexi
Grace
Seth
Levi

DIRECTOR'S NOTE: *Children may be called by their real names, if preferred.*

SETTING: *children's classroom*

PROPS: *quilt, snack food, a large banner that reads "One Week Later," Bible, baby blanket, toy, food, baby clothes, board books, piggy bank*

COSTUMES: *contemporary winter clothing*

Ms. Linda and the children sit on the quilt in a circle. Lexi munches on snack food throughout the scene.

Scene 1

MS. LINDA: Who knows what holiday we're celebrating?

All the children's hands fly in the air, and they start calling, "Christmas," with a few also saying, "Jesus' birthday."

MS. LINDA: That's right. We're celebrating Christmas, a day to remember Jesus' birth. We don't really know what day Jesus was born, but December twenty-fifth is the day we celebrate. I'm wondering, how does your family celebrate Christmas?

Children's hands go up.

MS. LINDA: Yes, Kelsey?

KELSEY: We put up a Christmas tree.

MS. LINDA: Great one. What about the rest of you? How many have a Christmas tree?

All raise their hands.

MS. LINDA: What else do you do for Jesus' birthday? Corey, what does your family do?

COREY: We bake a cake and sing "Happy Birthday" to Jesus.

MS. LINDA: Oh, I like that idea. Does anyone else do that?

Lexi and Grace raise their hands.

MS. LINDA: Wonderful! What else? Seth, what about your family?

SETH: We go to my grandma's house on Christmas Eve.

MS. LINDA: I'd say a lot of you visit relatives during Christmas, don't you?

Heads nod.

MS. LINDA: Levi, we haven't heard from you yet. What does your family do?

LEVI: We drive all over the place and look at all the Christmas lights. Have you seen the lights at the park? Wow! They're amazing! You've got to go see them. *(The longer he talks, the louder and faster he goes.)* They have Santa and Rudolph and the wise men and the shepherds and angels and baby Jesus in a manger and stars and elves and gingerbread people and—

MS. LINDA: *(laughing)* I think we get the picture, Levi. How many of you have seen the decorations at the park?

All hands go up.

MS. LINDA: Well, look at that, Levi. A lot of your friends enjoy those amazing lights too.

Levi nods his head enthusiastically.

MS. LINDA: What about other Christmas traditions?

KELSEY: We set out a nativ . . . a nativ . . . oh, you know, baby Jesus with Mary and Joseph and the sheep and everybody.

MS. LINDA: A nativity scene.

KELSEY: That's it, a nativity scene. Actually, we have several all over the house, and you know what?

MS. LINDA: What?

KELSEY: Instead of putting the wise men next to baby Jesus, we put them on the other side of the room. You know why?

MS. LINDA: *(smiling)* Why?

KELSEY: Because my daddy said the wise men had a long, long trip. He said Jesus was probably about two years old and living in a house before they ever found Him.

SETH: Wow, that is a long trip!

KELSEY: And they had to make it on camels too.

MS. LINDA: Your daddy's right, Kelsey. Although most people put their wise men next to baby Jesus, He probably was a little boy before they arrived. I may have to start your family's tradition with my nativity scene. I like that idea. *(pause)* If I remember correctly, everyone said you have a Christmas tree, right? What do you put under your tree?

ALL CHILDREN: Presents!

MS. LINDA: And who gets those presents?

ALL CHILDREN: We do!

MS. LINDA: Hmm. I'm a little confused. Whose birthday is it?

ALL CHILDREN: *(a little quieter)* Jesus.

MS. LINDA: And who gets the presents?

ALL CHILDREN: *(still quieter)* We do.

COREY: Ms. Linda, that's not right. If it's Jesus' birthday, why don't we buy gifts for Him?

MS. LINDA: Good question, Corey. *(looking around at the group)* Everyone, if you could have taken a gift to Jesus when He was born, what would you have taken? Kelsey, you start.

KELSEY: A warm blanket.

MS. LINDA: Great idea, Kelsey. Babies need to stay warm.

COREY: A toy.

MS. LINDA: Yes, all babies should have a toy, shouldn't they, Corey?

LEXI: Something to eat.

MS. LINDA: *(smiling)* Of course, Lexi. We all need to eat.

GRACE: Some clothes.

MS. LINDA: Good thinking, Grace. Jesus' mother wrapped Him in strips of cloth when He was first born, but we couldn't leave Him in those forever, could we?

SETH: Books, so Mary and Joseph could read to Him.

MS. LINDA: Don't you just love to read, Seth? And you know what? One of the best ways we learn to read is if our parents read to us when we're little.

LEXI: I would give Jesus' family some money, so they could find a better place to stay.

MS. LINDA: How thoughtful, Lexi. A stable provided Mary, Joseph, and baby Jesus shelter, but newborn babies definitely need a cleaner, safer place to live. *(Pause, looking around at everyone.)* I love all your gift ideas. Why don't you bring what you mentioned with you next week, and we'll give those gifts to Jesus?

GRACE: But Ms. Linda, how can we give them to Jesus? He lives in heaven.

MS. LINDA: Just trust me on this, okay, Grace? Bring your gifts next week, and we'll celebrate Jesus' birthday by giving all of them to Him.

Lights out.

Scene 2

Two children carry the banner reading "One Week Later" across the stage. Everyone returns to previous positions with their gifts.

MS. LINDA: Wonderful! You all remembered your gifts for Jesus. Before we give them to Him, I need a volunteer to read a verse from the Bible.

SETH: I will, Ms. Linda.

MS. LINDA: Thank you, Seth. *(Hand him an open Bible.)* Here you go. Read Matthew 25:40.

SETH: "The King will reply, 'Truly I tell you, whatever you did for one of the least of these brothers and sisters of mine, you did for me.'"

MS. LINDA: Who do you suppose "the King" is here?

SETH: Jesus?

MS. LINDA: You're exactly right, Seth. So what's Jesus telling us?

LEXI: *(uncertainly)* When we do something to help somebody in need, we're doing that for Jesus?

MS. LINDA: Absolutely, Lexi! So what do we need to do with the gifts we brought for Jesus?

LEXI: *(excited)* Give them to someone who needs them!

MS. LINDA: Right again! And when we do that, we are giving them to Jesus. Now, let's put our heads together and decide who will get these gifts for Jesus.

Everyone moves closer together and starts talking quietly.

Lights out.

Christmas Wrapping Paper Caper

by Alice Sullivan © 2015

SUMMARY: *While Mom is trying to wrap presents, she notices the wrapping paper keeps disappearing. The kids are wrapping themselves as gifts.*

CHARACTERS:
Mom
Dillon
Bree
Pips, the family dog

DIRECTOR'S NOTE: *Children may be called by their real names, if preferred.*

SETTING: *house with two rooms: one as a bedroom or kitchen, and the other a living room with Christmas decorations such as a tree. It is a few days before Christmas.*

PROPS: *dog (or child dressed as dog), tape dispensers, kid-friendly scissors (two pair), several tubes of wrapping paper, bows, table for wrapping gifts, boxes/gifts to wrap. If using a real dog, just let him roam free most of the skit until he needs to have a bow put on his/her head or around the neck. If a child dressed as a dog, he/she can follow the kids each time they go to Mom's room.*

COSTUMES: *contemporary winter clothing*

Scene 1

Mom is putting boxes of Christmas gifts on a table to prepare them to be wrapped. As she's deciding which gifts to wrap first and looking through her many rolls of wrapping paper, the kids are whispering to each other close by, planning their sneaky surprise.

MOM: *(humming Christmas carols to herself)* Look at all these great presents! I hope Dillon and Bree like what we got them. I can't wait to see what Santa brings everyone too! I know they've been good this year. *(She takes the biggest box first, selects some wrapping paper, and starts to cut it to size.)*

DILLON: *(to Bree)* Do you see that big box? I wonder what's in it. Maybe it's a puppy!

BREE: *(hushes Dillon)* Shhhh! Don't let Mom hear you. I bet it isn't a puppy. The box isn't jumping around. Maybe it is a new computer!

DILLON: No, no. Hey! Do you see that bag of bows on the table? I bet if we're quiet, you can grab the paper, I can grab the bag, and we can start wrapping Mom's gifts!

BREE: Okay! I'll go first! *(Bree crawls quietly to the table, reaches up, grabs a roll of wrapping paper, and crawls back to the other room.)*

DILLON: Great! Now we need some pretty bows! I'll get them. *(Dillon crawls to the table, grabs some bows, and quietly crawls back to the other room. Mom looks up, looks at the table, and seems confused.)*

MOM: Hmm. I thought I had more paper than this. *(Then she goes back to wrapping.)*

BREE: We have paper and bows, but how are we going to cut the paper?

DILLON: We need scissors! I think I saw an extra pair on the table. I'll be right back. *(Dillon belly crawls on the floor to the table like he's a spy, pops his hand up, feels around for the scissors, and comes back.)*

BREE: Yay! Now we have scissors! Wait . . . we don't have any tape! Can we use gum?

DILLON: No, I don't have enough gum. Plus, Pips would just eat it.

BREE: Okay, I'll go get the tape. *(She crawls to the table and takes the extra tape. She crawls back without being caught. Bree and Dillon disappear offstage with the supplies.)*

Scene 2

Mom is now on her second or third gift, and she notices she's running out of tape. She calls to the kids, but they don't answer. She's starting to get suspicious that they're up to something.

MOM: Bree? Dillon? Have you seen my tape? I had some extra tape right here *(She turns all the way around in a circle.)* . . . at least I thought I did. *(She looks under the table too.)* Guess I need to get some more tape out of the closet!

She walks offstage, and as she does, Dillon runs into the room and snatches another roll of paper. He is wearing a cape made of wrapping paper and a bow on his head, like a king. He leaves the room just as Mom walks back in.

DILLON: *(to Bree)* Whew! Got it! That was close!

MOM: *(looks down at the table)* Now how is that possible? I had another roll of paper right here! Maybe I'm just imagining things. I hope the kids aren't playing a trick on me. *(She goes back to wrapping gifts.)*

Scene 3

Mom is almost finished wrapping gifts but now needs more wrapping paper and goes offstage to grab another roll. As she does, Bree hops in, her legs wrapped together in paper . . . like a potato sack race. She grabs another roll and hops off just as Mom comes back to the room.

MOM: What in the world?! How is the paper disappearing? Kids! Are you taking my paper and tape and scissors? That's not a very nice thing to do. *(She walks into the other room to see the kids and the dog totally wrapped up in paper.)*

BREE AND DILLON: Surprise!

MOM: What is this?

BREE: We wanted to wrap Christmas presents for you!

DILLON: Yeah! And we are all we had!

BREE: Pips likes his bow! *(Pips can wear a bow on his head or a bow around his neck.)*

MOM: *(Hugging both kids close.)* You kids are the best gift a mom could have . . . and you did a very nice job of wrapping yourselves! *(looks at Pips)* You too, Pips! Next year you can wrap all the gifts!

Everyone walks off-stage. Lights out.

Youth

Christmas Mouse

by Diana C. Derringer © 2015

SUMMARY: *Some people speculate that a mouse damaged the organ in the Church of St. Nicholas in Oberndorf, Austria, prior to Christmas Eve in 1818. As a result, the church needed new music. If that is true and if that hungry mouse could talk, this may be how he would describe the origin of "Silent Night."*

CHARACTER: *Mouse*

SETTING: *church worship center*

PROPS: *a piece of cheese*

COSTUME: *mouse costume or gray clothing and a painted face*

Mouse enters, nibbling on a piece of cheese and speaking with much animation.

MOUSE: No one seems to know me. *(Throw hands in the air.)* I can't understand that. Everyone knows my cousins, several times removed, Mickey and Minnie, but not me. It doesn't make sense! *(hands on hips)* What have they ever done except dance around *(mimic dancing)* in funny clothes and act goofy? *(Smile and speak behind raised hand.)* No insult intended toward their good friend, of course. *(Lower hand, thumb to chest.)* But me . . . what would the world be without me? Christmas definitely would not be the same. Had it not been for me, *(Lean forward, hands on hips, and raise voice.)* there would be no "Silent Night"!

I'll bet you've never heard of Oberndorf either, have you? Okay, here's your geography lesson for today. Oberndorf is a village in Austria, near Salzburg. *(hands on hips and head cocked to the side)* You *(great emphasis)* have heard of Salzburg, haven't you? Actually, I lived in the Church of St. Nicholas in Oberndorf, a lovely church, not too big. The curate, Joseph Mohr, was only twenty-six in 1818, when my story begins.

It was Christmas Eve, see, and Joseph had just discovered that the church organ didn't work. I really hated that, too, because I knew what caused the problem. Winters get *(Hug self and shiver.)* extremely cold in Austria, and finding good mouse food becomes harder and harder. Sooo, being an enterprising young rodent, I discovered that some parts of an organ, although not very tasty, *(rubbing stomach)* can be quite filling. However, I wasn't about to jump up and say, *(Raise hand.)* "I did it." I may be little, but I'm not dumb! Instead, I stayed hidden to see what would happen next.

I had already learned that young curate was rather enterprising himself and talented as well. Not only could he preach, he wasn't half bad with a violin and guitar . . . not at the same time, of course. That particular Christmas Eve, I discovered he could also write. He handed a poem he had written a couple of years earlier to his good friend Franz Gruber, who set those words to music. And the rest, *(Extend arms to the sides and raise eyebrows.)* as they say, is history.

In spite of a broken organ, the music at Midnight Mass *(Put hands together beside face and tilt head, as in a swoon.)* was heavenly. If you ask me, I believe it was the best ever. With Father Mohr playing guitar and singing tenor, Franz Gruber singing bass, and the choir joining in at the refrains, why I thought I had died and gone on to mouse glory!

And now their song, *(greater emphasis and patting chest with both hands)* our song, continues as a part of Christmas celebrations all around the world. *(Extend arms to the sides.)* So, now you know.

Exit, nibbling on cheese as music to "Silent Night" begins.

Noel Motel

by Rob Britt

SUMMARY: *A contemporary telling of the Christmas story.*

CHARACTERS:
Desk Clerk, young adult male or female
Joe, young man
Mary, young woman, very pregnant
Mr. Smith, adult male
Ms. Smith, adult female
Jill, teenage female
Player, teenager
Coach, adult male
Dr. Shepherd, adult male
Shepherd family, adult female, two children
Wise Guy #1, adult male
Wise Guy #2, adult male
Wise Guy #3, adult male

SETTING: *small motel, gym/basketball court*

PROPS: *desk and chair, phone, luggage, motel room key, two cots, basketball rack and basketballs, baby doll wrapped in a blanket, gold necklace, gift certificate, stuffed bear*

COSTUMES: *business casual attire for the desk clerk, contemporary casual attire for travelers, workout clothing for basketball players and coach, casual camping attire for the doctor and family, contemporary clothing for the wise guys*

Scene 1

Joe and Mary Carpenter enter as the phone rings. They move slowly, as Mary is very pregnant.

DESK CLERK: Noel Motel, Bethlehem, Alabama. How may I help you? Rooms? Let's see. Sir, we have one room left. I'm sorry, sir, due to current demand, our rooms are first-come, first-served. Happy Holidays! *(Call ends.)* Merry Christmas . . . what's the big deal? Merry. Happy. Christmas. Well, Christmas is a holiday. I'm just covering my bases.

JOE: Hold on, Mary. I think I left my wallet in the car. *(Joe exits as Smith family enters and approaches the desk.)*

DESK CLERK: Noel Motel, how may I help you?

MR. SMITH: You still have vacancies, I hope?

DESK CLERK: We do.

MS. SMITH: I can't believe it. You're the last place in town with rooms.

DESK CLERK: It's one room, and now that's gone to you nice people. *(Hands Mr. Smith a key.)* Room 275 . . . through these elevators and down the hall on the right. Thank you for visiting the Noel Motel! *(Smiths exit as Joe and Mary approach.)*

JOE: A room, please.

DESK CLERK: I'm sorry, sir, but we're all booked up. We don't have rooms available.

JOE: But my wife's pregnant, and we've driven a long way. You've got to have something.

DESK CLERK: We have a small gym in the back. We put some cots on the basketball court in there last year for some hurricane evacuees, and they seemed to do okay. I can have housekeeping set you up with everything you need if you'd like.

JOE: Cots on a basketball court? Don't you have—

MARY: *(interrupting)* My feet say we'll take it.

JOE: But—

MARY: Joe, cots on a basketball court sound a whole lot nicer than feet on a hard lobby floor.

JOE: *(shrugs)* You heard her.

DESK CLERK: Follow me, please.

MARY: Uh-oh!

JOE: Uh-oh, what?

MARY: Joe, I think it's time.

JOE: Mary, now's not a good time.

MARY: Tell that to the baby.

Joe gets on one knee in front of Mary and talks to the baby.

JOE: Son, now is not a good time—

MARY: It doesn't work that way. *(to Desk Clerk)* Can they hurry up with one of those cots?

DESK CLERK: I'll get them right on it.

Scene 2

Scene changes to Joe and Mary sitting on a cot. There is a container holding basketballs in front of them, and a wrapped baby is nestled amongst them. A basketball player enters.

JILL: There's a baby in the basketballs.

JOE: It's my son. He wasn't due for a little longer, but he decided he was ready to see the world.

PLAYER: So cute . . .

Coach enters.

COACH: Jill, have you got those basketballs ready?

JILL: Dad, I can't.

COACH: Why not? The Bethlehem Angels can't practice without basketballs.

JILL: There's a baby in the basketballs.

COACH: Babies can't play basketball . . . they are too short.

JILL: Come see, but shhhh! He's sleeping. *(They move to Joe and Mary.)*

COACH: Congratulations, folks. I'm Coach Jones of the Angels basketball team. Do you have a doctor?

MARY: We are from out of town.

COACH: Jill, Amy's dad is a doctor, isn't he? Yeah, Dr. Shepherd . . . what's he doing tonight?

JILL: He wanted to do a back-to-nature Christmas Eve. All the Shepherds are camping in the field outside of town.

COACH: It's not far. Go tell him about the baby.

Jill exits as Desk Clerk enters.

DESK CLERK: How are we doing? Coach Jones . . . sorry about your gym.

COACH: This is much more important. Do you folks need anything while we wait for Dr. Shepherd?

Doctor and family enter with Jill.

DR. SHEPHERD: Here I am.

Three Wise Guys enter.

WISE GUY #1: They said behind the motel next to the Star Diner . . . looks like we are in the right place.

WISE GUY #2: The newborn baby is a bit unexpected.

DESK CLERK: I'm sorry. We are all out of rooms, and we have a bit of a situation.

WISE GUY #3: We have a reservation. We are the entertainment for the Christmas party.

DESK CLERK: Now I got it.

WISE GUY #1: We are the music and comedy team of the Three—

WISE GUY #2: Wise—

WISE GUY #3: Guys. You know, we need a gift for the baby. I've got my gold necklace!

WISE GUY #2: I've got that gift certificate from Frank's Incense.

WISE GUY #1: *(pulls a stuffed bear out of his bag)*—Murray!

WISE GUY #2: But you love that bear. You've had it since you were a baby.

WISE GUY #1: And now it's time to pass that love on.

Place bear next to baby. The Shepherds, the Three Wise Guys, and Jill and the Coach gather around the Carpenters and the baby. The Desk Clerk remains off to the side.

DESK CLERK: What a crazy Christmas Eve. I doubt anything like this has ever happened before. A baby born behind the motel, angels telling the Shepherds to come see it, and Three Wise Guys showing up with gifts. Oh, wait. I guess it has.

Lights fade.

Family Dinner

by Shayna DuPré

SUMMARY: *A family's discussion shows how distracted we get, causing us to lose the importance of Christmas.*

CHARACTERS:
Mother, adult female
Father, adult male
Son, teenage boy
Daughter, teenage girl

SETTING: *dining room table with four chairs*

PROPS: *dining room table, four chairs, food and silverware on table, two cell phones for teenagers, newspaper for Dad, food dish for Mom*

COSTUMES: *dressed casually for dinner*

Scene opens with Father and Son sitting at the table (Son is typing away on his phone). Mom walks up with a dish of food, and Daughter walks up talking on the phone.

DAUGHTER: Sarah, you wouldn't believe it! I'm telling you. I still can't believe he talked to me! His exact words were, "Hey. What time is it?" He is just so smart. And he chose me to ask what time it was!

MOM: Casey—get off the phone, please. *(As she sets down the dish.)*

DAD: As much as I love to hear about this knight in shining armor, listen to your mother, it's dinner time. And Josh, can we lose the games for enough time to at least eat with your family? *(As he folds up the newspaper, his son, begrudgingly, puts his phone in his pocket.)*

DAUGHTER: I'll fill you in on the rest later. Ciao. *(hangs up phone.)* All right, you've got my full attention, family, now what?

MOM: It would be nice if we said grace. It is Christmas after all; we have a lot to be thankful for. In fact, after grace, I was thinking we could go around and each say what we are grateful for.

SON: Mom, we just did that at Thanksgiving. Why should we do it again so soon?

MOM: Maybe because we were all just showered with gifts this morning and we have a lot to be thankful for.

DAD: Believe it or not, Thanksgiving isn't the only time of year to express gratitude, son.

SON: Fine, fine.

Everyone waits, looking at the dad.

DAD: What? Do you want me to start?

MOM: No, honey. Grace.

DAD: Oh, okay. All right, first, let's bow our heads. And, uh, hold hands? God, we umm, we are thankful for umm, everything. You have blessed us with food and family and gifts, and umm, we're grateful. Amen.

MOM: So, I'll start. *(As everyone starts eating, including her.)* I am grateful for a loving husband and two healthy children.

DAD: I am grateful for a roof over our heads and my wife, who has prepared such a wonderful meal.

SON: I'm grateful I got three new games and two iTunes gift cards.

DAUGHTER: Two iTunes gift cards? I only got one! Mom!

SON: My other one was from Jason, calm down.

MOM: Casey, you got so many gifts today—how could you possibly be mad?

DAUGHTER: I just wanted to make sure it's fair.

MOM AND DAD: Life isn't fair!

After the shouting, everyone is silent and just starts eating.

MOM: So, Casey, what are you grateful for?

DAUGHTER: *(Stays silently eating, just staring at her mom.)*

MOM: *(Puts fork and knife down.)* Is it too much to ask for one meal where we thank God for our gifts? Our health? Our home? And, maybe, each other?

DAUGHTER: I hear you, Mom, but Sarah is calling me back. *(Walks away as she answers the phone.)*

SON: Why do I have to be here if she doesn't? *(Stands up and walks away.)*

DAD: Maybe next Christmas will be different, honey. I don't know what to tell you.

MOM: I wish there was a way to connect with them. Show them how important family is and get them to understand there is more to this time of year than themselves. But, I guess there isn't. *(She gets up and walks away as her husband picks up the paper again.)*

Christmas Confusion

by Diana C. Derringer © 2015

SUMMARY: *An adult reminds a teen of the true meaning of Christmas.*

CHARACTERS:
Ms. Lora, adult church member
Drew, a hyperactive but lovable teenage boy

SETTING: *church worship center*

PROPS: *Christmas decorations, recorded Christmas music, Bible, glasses*

COSTUMES: *Santa hat with bells, contemporary winter clothing*

Christmas music plays until Ms. Lora enters, carrying a Bible. Then jingle bells ring, and Drew, wearing Santa hat with bells, appears singing.

DREW: Jingle bells, jingle bells . . . *(Look at audience with surprise before speaking.)* Whoa, Ms. Lora, a lot of those people out there are big! *(Pause and look again.)* A bunch of little bitty ones, too.

MS. LORA: That's okay, Drew. They're all friends who've joined us to celebrate Christmas. By the way, nice hat.

DREW: Thanks! I have the Christmas spirit! *(Become very animated.)* I've been decking the halls, buying gifts, hinting for my own gifts . . . ahem, hinting for my own gifts . . . *(Tilt head and gaze for a long time toward Ms. Lora.)*

MS. LORA: I get the hint, Drew. But that's not the true spirit of Christmas.

DREW: Oh, oh, I know! Santa and his sleigh, Rudolph and all those reindeer, Frosty . . . Hey, have you had a chance to check out my snowman and all the great lights on my house? Huh? Huh?

MS. LORA: Can't say that I have, Drew. But neither Santa and his reindeer, nor Frosty, nor any other snowmen show the true spirit of Christmas.

DREW: Okay, okay! I've got it now! It's stockings by the fireplace, hot chocolate and gingerbread men, families getting together, and *(sing)* music, music, music!

MS. LORA: All those are nice, but they're not why we celebrate Christmas either. Here, Drew, read this. *(Hand Drew Bible, opened to Luke 2.)* Verses 10 and 11.

DREW: Sure! No problem. *(Take the Bible, frown, then pull glasses from pocket and put them on with great ceremony. Exaggerate throat clearing.)* "But the angel said to them, 'Do not be afraid. I bring you good news that will cause great joy for all the people. Today in the town of David a Savior has been born to you; he is the Messiah, the Lord.'" *(calmer and more reverently)* Wow, I guess I kinda forgot about the heart of the Christmas story, didn't I?

MS. LORA: I'm afraid a lot of us do.

DREW: *(Return Bible.)* Well, gotta go! I need to remind my friends of the *(all in one breath and quickly)* official, number-one, genuine, absolutely correct, legitimate, hon-est-to-goodness, down-to-earth ... ha! ... Get it? ... down-to-earth? ... meaning of Christmas! Whadda'ya think?

MS. LORA: I think that's an excellent idea, Drew.

DREW: Thanks! See ya. *(Exit singing.)* We wish you a merry Christmas. We wish you a merry Christmas.

Lights out.

Angels Among Us

by Alice Sullivan © 2015

SUMMARY: *Two junior-high boys, once enemies, become friends as they realize what giving is all about.*

CHARACTERS:
Matt: quiet kid, wears big glasses
Breck: mean kid
Breck's friends: two or three boys
Children in hallway: also kids in background

DIRECTOR'S NOTE: *Children may be called by their real names, if preferred.*

SETTING: *school hallway, next to a wall or lockers*

PROPS: *big glasses for Matt, some pocket change for Matt, textbooks, one large envelope*

COSTUMES: *school clothes*

Scene 1

Matt is standing next to his locker with his arms full of books. Breck and his friends walk up, laughing loudly and standing together in an intimidating way.

BRECK: Hey Matt. Give me a dollar.

MATT: *(turn away, clutch books)* I don't have a dollar.

BRECK: *(step closer and push Matt's shoulder)* Yes, you do. You always have snack money. That's why we're friends!

Breck laughs back at his friends, who all laugh with him.

MATT: We're not friends. And I don't have any money.

BRECK: Did you spend it all on Kleenex so you can wipe your tears?

Breck's friends laugh. One calls Matt a "crybaby."

MATT: No. I didn't. I'm saving my money so I can help my family this Christmas.

BRECK: Oh? Are you gonna buy them a whole truckload of snacks?

MATT: No. I'm saving to buy my mom an angel necklace. Since my dad is still in the hospital from his work injury, Mom said we didn't have money for gifts this year, but I wanted to get her and my two little sisters something anyway. So I'm saving my money. You can go harass someone else.

Matt walks offstage. Breck's expression changes from being a bully to being concerned about Matt's family.

BRETT: *(turn to friends)* Hey guys, I didn't know Matt's dad was in the hospital. I feel bad for him. Every kid should be able to have a good Christmas *(boys agree)*.

ONE OF BRECK'S FRIENDS: Yeah, and it's really nice that he wants to get his mom an angel necklace.

ANOTHER OF BRECK'S FRIENDS: And toys for his sisters.

BRECK: Let's see what we can do!

Boys exit stage; lights go down.

Scene 2

Breck and his friends round up all the kids (Matt is still off-stage) to discuss his plan.

BRECK: Hey everyone! I have an announcement *(Hold up hands to get everyone's attention.)* Matt's dad is in the hospital and his mom told him they won't have Christmas this year. I think every kid should be able to have Christmas.

KID IN BACKGROUND: So what should we do?

BRECK: Maybe if we save our snack money for a week and put it together for him, he will have enough to buy gifts for his family.

ALL KIDS: Yeah! *(Some can say, "That's a great idea." "Count me in." One says, "I'll give up my allowance for a week to help out!")*

The kids continue to plan and nod in agreement, smiling as the lights go down.

Scene 3

It's been a week since the initial conversation between Matt and Breck. Matt is standing by his locker again, and Breck and his friends walk up. Behind him, the rest of the kids in the hallway step closer to see what happens.

BRECK: Hey Matt!

MATT: I still don't have any snack money. Go away.

BRECK: No . . . uh . . . I wasn't going to ask you for money today.

MATT: You weren't?

BRECK: No. Actually I . . . uh . . . I wanted to apologize. I didn't know your dad was in the hospital.

MATT: Oh. It's okay. He should be coming home next week. He'll be able to get back to work in a month or so. At least I hope so. *(Looks down. Voice is sad.)*

BRECK: Yeah . . . about that . . . I thought—

Kid in background coughs loudly to interrupt Breck taking all the credit.

BRECK: Right. We all thought it would be nice to save our money for a week and give it to you so you could buy gifts for your family.

MATT: *(in shock)* Really?

BRECK: Yeah. Here! *(Hand him the large envelope)*

MATT: *(looks inside)* Wow! There's enough here to get gifts for my sisters, a card for my dad, and even the angel necklace for my mom! I don't know what to say.

KID IN BACKGROUND: Say, "Thank you!"

MATT: Thank you. This really means a lot to me.

Breck holds his hand out to Matt, who shakes it and smiles.

BRECK: Merry Christmas, Matt.

MATT: Merry Christmas, Breck.

All kids cheer and lights fade.

Christmas Eve Shopping

by Shayna DuPré

SUMMARY: *A woman and her child are waiting in line at a retail store when she gets a call from her friend.*

CHARACTERS:
Mom, adult female
Child, could be boy or girl
Various other patrons in line

SETTING: *retail desk with two clerks and two lines of customers with Mom and Child at the end of one*

PROPS: *retail desk with computers or cash registers on counter, several items (or an overloaded shopping basket) and a cell phone for Mom*

COSTUMES: *dressed casually for a day of shopping*

Scene opens with our main character holding her child's hand while trying to balance everything else and decide which line to get in.

Both lines have several people in them, but one is slightly shorter than the other. Before dialogue begins, she stands in one that doesn't move, so she moves to the other. As she does, the other line begins moving, so she switches back, only to watch the other one start moving again. She decides to stay where she is. The other customers in line are chatting and looking at their purchases. Finally, her phone rings.

MOM: Where is my phone, where is my phone? *(look around frantically)* Why can't anything be easy today? . . . I'm coming! Coming! Oh, here it is. Hello, hello? Hey, Diane. No, no, I'm shopping now. I know, leave it to me to STILL have shopping to do on Christmas Eve. And my babysitter fell through, so I have Charley here with me too. *(Child wanders to look at something.)* Charley! Stay over here! Don't make this errand harder than it has to be! And why, Diane, why do I always, without fail, choose the wrong line?! Everywhere I go . . . the bank, the grocery, I have a curse! Between picking up dinner, which I barely got there before they closed. Speaking of, why do grocery stores close early on Christmas Eve? You chose to work there; it's not my fault if that means working holidays. And then, John calls to tell me I have already gone over budget with shopping this year. Of course, that didn't change anything. I am just using credit cards and will ask for forgiveness later. I'm not sure how he thinks I can buy gifts for his entire family, my entire family, our kids, and each other without going into a little bit of debt . . . although I am not even sure we have paid off last year's debt yet. But, hey, it's what this time of year is about, right? *(Both lines are slowly moving forward during the call.)* Racking up credit card bills, cooking nonstop, running from party to party, wrapping gifts until 2 a.m., only to be woken up by 5 a.m., when I don't even enjoy the *(whisper here)* happiness on my kids' faces because I am barely keeping my eyes open. Oh yes—this truly is the most magical time of year! And then the Andersons' party tomorrow—oh no, I have to make a casserole! I forgot to get the ingredients at the store—do you know if any place is open tomorrow? Ugh, if not, I am sure I can bake some cookies or something. I'll call Kathleen to make sure it's okay. This is just what I need—add something else to the to-do list!

CHILD: Mom, Mom, church. What about church? You forgot to tell her we have that tonight too.

MOM: What, honey? Oh, Christmas Eve service at church. Ha. I completely forgot about that. Well, we don't have time to do everything. I just don't think we are going to have time this year, sweetheart.

Anyway, Diane, have you bought teacher's gifts yet? I'll have to do gift cards again. I mean, who has the time to get everything done? All I know is I hope I am teaching my kids how to get through the holidays. It's not easy, and if I don't show them, then who will?

(The line finally shortens and she is one person away.)

Listen, I've got to let you go. Sorry to bother you . . . oh wait, you called me, right? Oh, there is something you wanted to tell me? Can it wait? It's my turn—I'll call you back . . . well, sometime! You know how it is . . . I've just got so much to do. So, I'll talk to you soon—bye!

(To the clerk) Hi, there. Merry Christmas!

The Unexpected King

by Rob Britt

SUMMARY: *Three men prepare to bring gifts to the King. They discuss the best gifts while not truly understanding who the gifts are for or what would be appropriate.*

#1: A ring. A beautiful, shiny ring.

#2: A palace. With towers that reach to the heavens, and a throne room as big as all outdoors with sweet fragrances in the air. The king will sit and make decisions that will change the world.

#1 and #2 look at #3, but his expression doesn't change.

#1: Well, if there's going to be a king, I'm thinking too small. A chain, yes, that's it. A chain to be worn around the king's neck, and people will come from miles around to be allowed to take a glance.

#2: We are both thinking small. Why be as big as all outdoors when you can be outdoors? Let the beasts themselves enjoy the fragrance. This king has come to save, so there will be battles. After each victory, he will relax in his vast tent and plan the next day's campaign. The fragrances will give him a clear head. His plans will be perfect, and victory will be assured.

#1 and #2 look at #3, but his expression still doesn't change.

#1: *(to #2)* Quiet one, huh?

#2: I should say so.

#1: He's just missing all the fun.

#3 looks engaged in the conversation for the first time.

#3: You're right. There's not a lot of laughing when I'm around.

#1: No wonder. You're depressing. *(excited again)* Wait! I got it. The king's chariot—the one he rides into all those victories you help him plan. His enemies will know that the king is coming when they see his chariot, and they will see it from miles away. It will reflect the sun so brightly that people will have to shield their eyes. The king's war machine of wood and—

#3: There will be wood, but it won't be a chariot. It will look more like this—*(He starts to do something with his arms, but #2 cuts him off.)*

#2: Excuse me, sir. Must you be so negative? My friend and I are celebrating our future in the service to a king.

#3: I will serve a king as well.

#1: What are you?

#3: I am aromatic resin of a number of small, thorny tree species of the genus Commiphora. You might know me as—

All 3 characters react as if they've been jostled all at once.

#1: I think we've stopped.

#2: You know what that means?

#1: We're at the palace! We are gifts to the king!

#1 and #2 look shocked.

#2: That's quite unexpected.

#1: What's that smell?

#3: He's quite a lovely child. It's a shame I even have to be here.

#2: Why do you have to be here?

#1: Why do any of us? This isn't a palace. It's a very unremarkable house. There's no place to park a chariot.

#2: I don't believe we are in the presence of a king. There must be some mistake.

#3: There's no mistake.

#1: Oh, gross. The kid is smudging me. Now I will never reflect the sun.

#3: You just did.

#2: Would you stop being so mysterious? What did you say you were?

#1: Something's happening.

#2: They are bowing to the child. Can't they see this is no king? In this small, plain house.

#3: No, He's not *a* king . . . He's THE King!

#1: The one who has come to free Israel from the Romans?

#3: The one who has come to free all mankind from death.

#2: My heavens . . . literally.

#3: Hello, I'm Myrrh.

#1: Myrrh! That's used in the burial of the dead. This child will die!

#3: The child will see manhood, but the man will die.

#2: Why?

#3: Because He's not the king you've been talking about. He won't wear gold or burn the finest frankincense in any palace. He will travel about, on foot, for three years performing miracles in the name of His Father, Jehovah. He will show wisdom like none have seen before. He will love mankind like none have before. Those who choose not to believe will have Him put to death on a cross of wood.

#1: That's what you meant.

#2: That's where you come in.

#3: Yes, but it won't be for long.

#2: You are a burial powder. You stay where you are put.

#3: Not this time. In three days, I will be cast aside amongst the wrappings. The man will arise and leave the tomb. He will beat death. Because He will, anyone who believes this man is the Son of God, and who believes that He did beat death, will go to heaven when they pass from this earth.

#2: What is His name?

#1: His mother calls Him "Jesus."

Each character drops to their knees as they say their final line.

#1: Gold for the King of Kings!

#2: Frankincense for the wisest King!

#3: Myrrh for the King who will die, then return, so that all can be saved and come to know His Father!

Lights fade.

Not the Same Old Story

by Carlton W. Hughes © 2015

SUMMARY: *A Sunday school teacher tries to act cool to his youth students but has trouble controlling them during a session right before Christmas. The students think they know everything about the Christmas story, but through a rapid-fire quiz, the teacher shows them there's more to the story.*

CHARACTERS:
Mr. David, teacher
Youth:
Joy
Ashley
Megan
Harvey
Billy

DIRECTOR'S NOTE: *Teens may be called by their real names, if preferred.*

SETTING: *Sunday school classroom*

PROPS: *simple staging with chairs for the Sunday school students and possibly a podium for the teacher; Bible and bag of peppermint candy canes for Mr. David; students can also have Bibles and/or notepads and pencils; optional Christmas decorations around the room.*

Students are milling around a Sunday school classroom, talking and having fun. Mr. David enters, carrying Bible and bag of candy canes. He goes to the podium.

MR. DAVID: *(trying desperately to act cool to the kids)* What's up?!

Students pause for a moment, barely acknowledge Mr. David, and then return to their conversations with each other.

JOY: *(to Mr. David)* Not much, Mr. David. *(giggles, turns toward Ashley)* Ashley, I'm so glad school is finally on Christmas break—sleeping in every day for two whole weeks! That's heaven!

ASHLEY: Yeah, Joy, and I can't wait until Christmas. I just know Mom and Dad are getting me that new phone.

MR. DAVID: *(interrupting)* That's funky fresh, girls, but it's time to start our lesson.

HARVEY: *(ignoring Mr. David)* New phone—ha! *(to Billy)* Hey, Billy—I'm getting a new dirt bike from my parents!

BILLY: No way!

HARVEY: Wanna bet? *(Flips Ashley on the head.)*

ASHLEY: Stop it, Harvey!

MR. DAVID: *(Pulling out candy canes, trying to get kids' attention.)* I have some rad candy canes! *(Kids ignore him.)* REAL peppermint, not the janky fruity ones! *(They still ignore him.)*

MEGAN: Well, while you are all FREEZING, I'll be on the BEACH in FLORIDA! You'll be soooo JEALOUS when you see me at school . . . with my TAN . . . in JAN! *(Harvey pulls her hair.)* Mr. David, make Harvey stop!

MR. DAVID: *(taking charge)* Homies—SETTLE DOWN! Harvey—keep yo' hands to yo'self! *(Kids roll their eyes, make gestures like Mr. David is very uncool.)* The rest of the posse—get a SEAT and get QUIET! *(They sit down.)* You seem to be pumped for Christmas, but today our lesson is about the REAL REASON for the—

MEGAN: *(whining)* Ugh! We know this story!

BILLY: Megan's right, I've heard it over and over . . . Mary was the virgin girl . . .

HARVEY: And Joseph was her feller . . .

JOY: No room at the inn . . . blah, blah, blah!

HARVEY: That's it! Let's go have a snowball fight, boys versus girls! *(jumps up, and other kids follow, start to run out)*

MR. DAVID: Yo, yo, yo—get back here! *(Kids return to their seats.)* It seems like the same old story, but Christmas is just the beginning of the greatest story ever told.

ASHLEY: *(getting up)* I thought the greatest story ever told was Romeo and Juliet, when they fell in love, and everyone was fighting.

MR. DAVID: No. It is about God sending the greatest Gift ever to Earth . . . and it took a lot to get Jesus born.

MEGAN: *(getting interested)* Did Mary have problems or something?

MR. DAVID: No, but since you know this story, let's have some competition—boys versus girls. *(Sounds like a game show host.)* First, where was Jesus born?

HARVEY: Bethlehem!

MR. DAVID: Right, but Mary and Joseph had to travel miles and miles to be counted in the census, right when Mary was ready to have the baby. Next, how did they get there?

BILLY: Joseph's sweet red Corvette!

MEGAN: No, silly! A donkey!

JOY: To think, she had to ride that thing while she was in that condition.

MR. DAVID: Imagine how that must have felt. Next question, how old was Mary?

ASHLEY: Twenty-five!

HARVEY: Thirty!

MR. DAVID: Both wrong. Mary was the same age as all of you, in her teens.

MEGAN: I thought I have it bad, worrying about Algebra.

BILLY: Or if Donnie is going to call. *(makes kissing noises)*

MEGAN: Stop it, Billy!

MR. DAVID: A-ight. *(slang for "all right," pronounced "I eat.")* Final question: What place did Jesus leave to come here?

JOY: Nazareth!

HARVEY: No! Heaven?

MR. DAVID: Right, Harvey.

ASHLEY: I never thought about it before—Jesus CHOSE to leave heaven.

MEGAN: To be born in a stable.

MR. DAVID: Stables can be pretty janky.

BILLY: *(holding nose)* P-U! They're stinky!

JOY: Jesus became a helpless little baby?

MR. DAVID: The point of the story is that the King of Kings left the glory of heaven to experience what we experience.

HARVEY: Even pimples?

MR. DAVID: *(laughs)* Yes, I guess so. He did it all for me and for you . . . to save us all.

MEGAN: Wow, that is the greatest story ever.

MR. DAVID: Told you it wasn't the same old story, homies!

Lights fade out.

Adults

Tree Talk

by Diana C. Derringer © 2015

SUMMARY: *A woman reminisces while removing ornaments from her Christmas tree.*

CHARACTER: *Woman, middle age*

SETTING: *a family room*

PROPS: *an ornament box on a table and a Christmas tree with the following ornaments remaining: a nativity scene, a candy cane, an ornament from another country, a sprig of holly, and a cross*

COSTUME: *casual contemporary clothing*

Woman stands with hands on hips before the tree.

WOMAN: Well, old girl, you've done it again! You provide one of the best witnessing tools I know. Do you remember our refugee friends a few years ago? After years of hearing anti-Christian propaganda, they slowly relaxed as we shared and compared favorite foods and traditions. How they loved decorating you! *(Remove and hold nativity ornament.)* Ah, here was their favorite. This little manger scene and the story of no room for baby Jesus brought tears to their eyes. They understood far better than anyone I know how Mary and Joseph must have felt. What

66

joy to give them their own small tree with a nativity scene included among their box of ornaments. *(Place ornament in box.)*

My, who can forget this one? *(Remove and hold the candy cane.)* When little Jessie first saw it, *(laughing)* she wanted to eat it, so I gave her a real candy cane. While she munched, we reviewed its symbolism—the red for Jesus' shed blood; white for cleansing, offered to anyone who believes; and the shape either for Jesus *(Hold showing the J shape.)* or a shepherd's staff. *(Turn the cane over.)* She loved the idea of Jesus as her shepherd. *(Place candy cane in box.)*

Woman removes ornament from another country.

What memories this one carries from our first mission trip. By sharing the highlights of that trip, I hope I challenge others to pray, give, and go on a mission trip. So many people need to hear the good news of Jesus. *(Place ornament in box.)*

I can't resist including at least one sprig of holly every year. *(Remove holly.)* Such an easy way to tell of Jesus' suffering for us, the crown of thorns that pierced His head, and the blood He willingly shed so we might have forgiveness and abundant life. *(Place holly in box.)*

And my favorite! *(Remove cross.)* I wish I had a nickel for everyone who asked why I hang a cross on my Christmas tree. But we need to remember why Jesus came. I'm afraid we often leave Jesus in the manger, never recognizing the reason we celebrate. Without His death, burial, and resurrection, His birth would be meaningless. *(Place cross in box.)*

(Hands on hips, gazing at tree.) Now, my friend, away you go for another year. But I thank you for all your symbols—the lights that proclaim Jesus as light of the world and how we must reflect Him in an increasingly dark time, your lovely evergreen branches proclaiming eternal life possible through Jesus' gift of salvation . . . How I wish everyone knew His truth. But we'll keep telling, won't we? We'll keep telling.

Woman exits with box.

My App Has an App for That

by Shayna DuPré

SUMMARY: *A mom asks her daughter what she wants for Christmas.*

CHARACTERS:
Mother, adult female
Daughter, middle school or high school girl

SETTING: *a couch*

PROPS: *couch, notebook/pen, cell phone, headphones*

COSTUMES: *casual contemporary clothing*

Scene opens with Mother making a list, looking busy, and Daughter casually typing on her phone.

MOTHER: Sarah . . . (*Daughter keeps typing*) Sarah . . . (*still typing*) (*now shouting*) SARAH!!

DAUGHTER: (*pulling out one earbud, sounding exasperated*) What?

MOTHER: Attitude, please!

DAUGHTER: Sorry . . . (*muttering*) but you did interrupt me.

MOTHER: I'm going to pretend I didn't hear that. Now, what I was trying to do was ask you, darling daughter, what you want for Christmas this year.

DAUGHTER: *(suddenly smiling and much happier)* Ohhh, *(pulling out the other headphone)* why didn't you say so? *(still typing away though)*.

MOTHER: I have my annual Christmas book out—if you would lift your gaze from these gadgets for one millisecond, you would see that. And by now you know that when the book comes out, the lists go in! It's the only way I can stay organized while making sure I don't repeat gift anyone—or worse—re-gift to the giftee! Nope, this book keeps me on track year after year.

DAUGHTER: Mom, that book is so old. Get with the times: I'm sure there is an app for that.

MOTHER: There is probably an app for that app! And then an app for that app! You kids and your insta-skype . . .

DAUGHTER: *(muttering)* Instagram.

MOTHER: —fluttering—

DAUGHTER: Tweeting.

MOTHER: Swapchaps—

DAUGHTER: Snapchat.

MOTHER: I'm not sure how you keep up with every new trend coming your way. I just got the Facebook myself.

DAUGHTER: Please don't call it that.

MOTHER: Anyway, what new technology will you be asking for this year? Let's see, it looks like last year you asked for the newest iPad, a GoPro, and, oh yes, let's not forget—a selfie stick. And the year before—

(A paper falls out as she is browsing the book . . . Daughter finally looks away from her phone and picks up the paper.)

Yeah, it looks like the past three years the only items on your list either start with an "i" or are some sort of technology I don't even understand. Though honestly, Sarah, I don't even remember the last time we talked when you weren't texting or reading or photoshopping something, so can you at least try to ask for something different this year? *Mother isn't looking away from the book and Daughter is still reading the paper.)* Silence, huh? I know, I know, "I don't get it," umm, "I'm old," uh, what's the latest one, "if you grew up in this generation you would know why this all matters," and—*(She is interrupted as her daughter hugs her, crying.)*

Sarah, what the? Are you okay?

DAUGHTER: Mom, I love you. All I want this year is to spend time with you and bake cookies like we used to and go see the lights . . . remember how we used to do that?

MOTHER: Ohh, oh, Sarah. *(Knowing what Sarah must have read, she picks up the letter and starts reading it.)*

"Dear Santa, all I want for Christmas is my mommy to be healthy again. Nothing else in the world matters to me, and if you could get that wish to come true, I promise you won't ever get a letter from me again. Love, Sarah."

DAUGHTER: I didn't know you kept that, Mom.

MOTHER: I told you, I keep all of your lists. And just because you wrote that to Santa doesn't mean God didn't hear it as your prayer.

DAUGHTER: I sometimes forget what really matters, Mom. I'm sorry. God gave me the best gift that year. And that was before I even knew what FaceTime was.

MOTHER: *(Now she is muttering.)* I still don't . . .

DAUGHTER: But tonight, no cell phones. No computers. Just us.

MOTHER: That sounds good to me.

DAUGHTER: *(As they walk away arm in arm.)* But Mom, can we pull out the book later, because there is this new camera *(The mom stops and looks at her.)* . . . ummm . . . we can talk about it later. *(They walk and she lays her head on her mom's shoulder.)*

Buttons and Behavior

by Diana C. Derringer © 2015

SUMMARY: *A store clerk voices her thoughts about a common Christmas sentiment.*

CHARACTER: *Clerk, adult female*

SETTING: *store check out counter*

PROPS: *cash register on a table*

COSTUME: *contemporary clothing, hair slightly out of place*

Clerk observes an imaginary customer in a distant part of the store while totaling another person's purchase. She's moving her hands as though scanning barcodes and placing items in bags.

CLERK: Not another "Keep Christ in Christmas" button! Every year we go through the same old thing—buttons, shirts, signs, letters to the editor, even emails declaring we should keep Christ in Christmas. I don't have any problem with that. I enjoy a good "Merry Christmas" as well as anyone. But what about the rest of the year, and what about the actions of people who wear those shirts and buttons? I do believe some of their faces would break if they tried to smile. And how they push and shove their way through crowds! I know they're busy and tired, but who isn't? *(Wipe brow with back of wrist.)* By the time my shift ends, my feet feel like they might fall right off my legs, but I still have to finish my own shopping before I pick up the kids, fix their dinner, help with baths and homework, referee quarrels and fights, and get everything and everybody ready for the next day. *(Shake head and wipe eyes.)*

(Look to the side, point, and respond to an imaginary question.) Second aisle on the left near the bottom.

(Turn back to imaginary customer.) Sorry about that. As I was saying, I could use a little Christmas cheer myself . . . and not the kind in a bottle. My husband's had more than his fair share of that, thank you very much, and I have the bruises to prove it!

A few folks who go to that big church in town really seem happy. No, it's more than happy. I don't know how to explain it, but I sure wish I had some of it. Maybe someday one of them will take the time to tell me what makes the difference.

(Check total for customer.) Eighty-seven, thirty-five, please. *(Take imaginary money, place it in cash register, and hand imaginary receipt to customer.)* Thank you for shopping with us. *(Turn away, then look back and smile.)* Thank you, and Merry Christmas to you too!

Lights out.

Merry Memories

by Alice Sullivan © 2015

SUMMARY: *It's Christmas morning with the entire extended family, and all the adults are sitting around talking and sharing memories while the kids are opening presents.*

CHARACTERS:

Uncle Joe
Aunt Betty
Grandpa Miller
Grandma Miller
Granny Jean (whose husband has passed away)
Kids (several kids to play around the tree and unwrap gifts)
Mom
Dad

DIRECTOR'S NOTE: *Children and adults may be called by their real names, if preferred.*

SETTING: *living room with fireplace and tree (if possible)*

PROPS: *fake fireplace, chairs for adults, gifts for kids to unwrap, a few photo albums for adults to pass around (audience won't need to see contents)*

COSTUMES: *contemporary casual clothing*

Uncle Joe and Aunt Betty have just arrived with gifts and greet the rest of the family in the living room, just before the kids open presents.

UNCLE JOE AND AUNT BETTY: Merry Christmas, everyone!

KIDS: They're here! *(Hug Uncle Joe and Aunt Betty and get packages to put by the tree.)* Now we can open gifts!

GRANDMA MILLER: Yes! Everyone is here now, so Christmas festivities can begin. *(Adults all hug each other and share greetings. Kids all play together around the gifts.)*

GRANDPA MILLER: I saved you both some seats right next to Granny Jean. *(Uncle Joe and Aunt Betty sit next to Granny Jean and share hellos.)*

GRANNY JEAN: My, oh my. I just love the sound of Christmas morning. It reminds me of growing up on the farm when all the family would gather together and Mama and Daddy would make the biggest pancake breakfast! We had scrambled eggs, bacon, cat-head biscuits, sausage and gravy, and the biggest pancakes you ever did see!

KIDS: Cat-head biscuits? What's that?

GRANNY JEAN: It's a biscuit as big as a cat's head! That's what. Delicious! *(All laugh.)*

MOM: Grandma Miller, what was Christmas like for you growing up?

GRANDMA MILLER: Well, we never had much. But we had each other, and that was enough. My oldest brother, Joe, was in the Army during World War II, and we weren't sure if we'd ever see him again. When it came Christmastime in 1944, Mama was so worried because we hadn't received a letter from him in some time. We had all settled down to open gifts when there was a knock at the door. We weren't expecting anyone and it gave Mama quite a shock. I ran to open it and it was Santa Claus! I was about as surprised as a seven-year-old could be. He walked in, big white beard, red suit, big black boots, and a sack of toys for me and my other siblings—all six of us. He winked at Daddy then walked right over to Mama, wrapped her in a big hug, and said, "Merry Christmas, Mama! I'm home!" It was Joe, all dressed up, home from war. Lord, Mama about died! She couldn't decide whether to laugh or cry, so she did both and we did too! That was the happiest Christmas I recall.

GRANDPA MILLER: That reminds me of when my Uncle Jimmy dressed up as Santa and tried to wiggle down the chimney one year, but he was a big man and quickly realized he wouldn't fit. So then he thought he'd sneak in through a window while we were all still asleep, which would have worked, except that he chose the window right over our dog's sleeping spot. Ole' Rambler grabbed onto Jimmy's coat and wouldn't let go. We all awoke to Jimmy yelling for Rambler to let him go. By the time Mama and Daddy flipped on the lights in the kitchen and all us kids ran downstairs, Rambler was sitting on Jimmy, who was face down on the floor, like he was king of the mountain. Jimmy sure was mad, but Daddy was laughing so hard he couldn't even talk.

KIDS: Your Uncle Jimmy is Santa Claus?

GRANDPA MILLER: No, no. He was just a poor planner! *(All laugh.)*

AUNT BETTY: Well, my favorite Christmas tradition growing up was walking around to all the neighbors' houses and singing Christmas carols.

UNCLE JOE: That's my favorite memory too!

AUNT BETTY: It is? Why?

UNCLE JOE: Because that's how we met! *(turns to tell the story to the others)* I remember it like it was yesterday. Christmas Eve, 1964. We'd just set out all the presents when we heard singing outside and rushed to the windows. There was a group of carolers, each holding a candle, and singing the most wonderful songs. When the group started to sing "Silent Night," one pretty voice stood out from the rest and sounded like an angel singing. It was dark outside by then, and all I could see were her eyes and her nose from the candlelight as she sang, but I was in love right then. Asked her on our very first date that night.

AUNT BETTY: *(grabs Uncle Joe's hand)* And we've been together ever since!

DAD: *(grabs Mom's hand)* Speaking of Christmas memories, I think we should make one right here and teach the kids our favorite Christmas carols!

MOM: That's a great idea! Aunt Betty, will you start?

AUNT BETTY: I'd love to!

All sing "Silent Night." Kids come over and join in.

Lights fade.

Outside the Box

by Diana C. Derringer © 2015

SUMMARY: *Two young mothers learn from their children that we find the most important gifts outside a box.*

CHARACTERS:
Erica, young mother
Anna, young mother
Ethan, small boy
Adam, small boy

SETTING: *a family room*

PROPS: *small couch, Christmas tree, large cardboard box, toys, gift boxes, wrapping paper, bows*

COSTUMES: *contemporary winter clothing*

Erica and Anna sit on a couch next to a Christmas tree. Ethan and Adam laugh and play inside a cardboard box on the other side of the tree. Toys, gift boxes, wrapping paper, and bows lay scattered near the boys.

ERICA: *(laughing and shaking her head)* Will you look at those two. With every kind of toy a child could want, what do they play with? A cardboard box.

ANNA: *(laughing)* That's the way it goes. We make ourselves crazy trying to find the latest toy on the market when, most of the time, the boys couldn't care less.

ETHAN: *(yelling across the room)* Look at this, Mom. *(tossing bows in the air)* It's snowing!

ADAM: *(begins tossing bows too)* Yeah, it's snowing bow flakes! *(Ethan and Adam dissolve into giggles while Erica and Anna laugh and shake their heads.)*

ERICA: See, that's what I mean. *(staring at the boys and growing more solemn)* How I wish I could be that carefree again.

ANNA: Don't I hear you! By the time I finish all my chores at night, I'm as tired and grumpy as a hibernating bear with insomnia.

ERICA: *(laughing)* I never heard that expression before, but that's exactly what I mean. And it gets worse this time of year.

ANNA: I know! The extra shopping and cooking, the school parties—

ERICA: —with four dozen cookies to be baked for the next day. Plus, Ethan fails to tell me until I tuck him in for the night!

ANNA: Been there and done that one too!

ERICA: So many gifts to buy—

ANNA: —with so many bills to pay.

ERICA: Every year I tell myself I'm not charging any more than I can pay at the end of the month. Yet, every year I buy more than I plan and can't get the debt paid until it's time to start all over again. It's crazy! I'm crazy!

ANNA: Why do we do that? We're burying ourselves in a mountain of debt, buying things for one another we don't need and often don't want. We shower the kids with more toys than they can possibly play with, and then look *(pointing at Ethan and Adam)* at what they do.

ERICA: You know, I received only one or two gifts as a child at Christmas, and I was tickled to death.

ANNA: So was I, and I think I appreciated what I received more than most children today.

ERICA: Another thing: I have a friend who donates money in people's honor rather than driving herself nuts trying to think of gifts to buy for them.

ANNA: Hmm. I kind of like that idea.

Ethan gets out of the box and begins dragging Adam offstage. Erica and Anna watch them leave and smile. Suddenly a crash occurs offstage, and both boys run to Erica and Anna, crying.

ETHAN: *(throwing himself into Erica's arms)* The box broke, Mommy, and Adam fell out!

ANNA: *(checking Adam all over)* Are you hurt anywhere, sweetie?

ADAM: *(still crying)* The box broke. Now we don't have anything to play with.

Erica and Anna burst into laughter.

ANNA: Can you believe it? This floor is covered with toys, and they wonder what they will play with when their box tears up.

ADAM: It's not funny, Mommy!

ANNA: *(more seriously)* I'm sorry your box broke, honey. Why don't you and Ethan play with some of these toys instead. *(patting him)* Go on, now. See what you can find.

Ethan and Adam look at one another, shrug their shoulders, and begin playing with toys on the floor.

ANNA: You know, Erica, I think the boys just taught us an important lesson.

ERICA: What's that?

ANNA: We get all bent out of shape about what we will buy and how much we will spend on everyone, when none of that really matters. The boxes and bows and what's inside them are unimportant. What really counts is what's outside the box.

ERICA: Like family and friends—

ANNA: —and helping those in need—

ERICA: —and donating money where it's really needed instead of splurging on ourselves—

ANNA: —and sharing our greatest gift, *(pause)* the Christ of Christmas.

Lights out.

What Money Can't Buy

by Alice Sullivan © 2015

SUMMARY: *In the middle of a shopping spree, a family learns that the real treasure of Christmas is spending it with family—not the false message of buying many gifts.*

CHARACTERS:
Addie: youngest daughter, has a teddy bear
Cooper: middle child
Megan: oldest daughter
Mom
Dad

DIRECTOR'S NOTE: *Children may be called by their real names, if preferred.*

SETTING: *shopping center or mall (stage with two different entrances)*

PROPS: *long lists and markers for each person (except Addie), teddy bear for Addie, a large shopping bag full of packages for each person (can be cardboard boxes or crumpled paper), large nativity scene with lamb*

COSTUMES: *contemporary winter clothing*

Scene 1

Family is standing together in the food court, reviewing all the gifts they need to buy, checking off items from lists.

MOM: Megan and I will get the gifts for your mother, Aunt Leslie, Cousin Susan, our dog walker, Megan and Cooper's teachers, and . . . who are we forgetting?

ADDIE: Me!

MOM: Oh yeah. And Addie! *(pats Addie's head)*

ADDIE: Mommy, can we see baby Jesus?

MOM: Later, dear. We have to buy gifts first!

DAD: Great. We'll get the gifts for Uncle James, Cousin Mike, check out the new video games at the electronics store, get something for the mailman—

COOPER: The mailman?

DAD: That's what it says on my list.

MOM: Yes, the mailman. It's to make up for last year when Rusty got out of his kennel and chased the poor mailman up the tree.

Dad and Connor laugh.

MOM: It wasn't funny!

CONNOR: *(under his breath)* Yes, it was!

ADDIE: Mommy, can we see baby Jesus too?

MEGAN: *(pats her head, dismissing her)* Later, Addie!

Parents and older kids start comparing notes and talking all at the same time, ignoring Addie.

MOM: Okay! We'll meet back here in two hours! Let the games begin!

Everyone runs off to start shopping. Mom and Megan go one way. Dad and Cooper go another. Addie is left in the middle of the food court alone, holding her teddy bear.

ADDIE: *(looks one way)* Mom? *(looks the other way)* Dad? *(holds teddy bear tighter)* I just wanted to see baby Jesus.

Addie walks off-stage, lights go down.

Scene 2

Mom and Dad are frantically talking to each other on cell phones after realizing they lost Addie.

MOM: *(comes in stage left with Megan while on phone)* I thought you had her!

DAD: *(comes in stage right with Cooper while on phone)* No! I thought you had her!

COOPER: Where would she have gone?

MEGAN: *(remembers Addie's request)* Guys! She wanted to see baby Jesus! We have to find baby Jesus!

MOM: Do they have a manger scene here?

DAD: We're going to find out! *(to Mom)* You and Megan go that way. We'll go this way! *(with Cooper)* Call immediately if you find her!

All run off stage, calling to Addie.

Scene 3

Addie finds the manger scene and walks over to baby Jesus.

ADDIE: Hello, baby Jesus! I wanted to come see you, but my family wanted to buy gifts. Christmas must be all about spending money. But now I'm all alone. Me and my bear. I hope they find me soon. *(looks around for her family)* You don't mind if I stay here with your family, do you?

Addie curls up next to a lamb and takes a nap.

Scene 4

Mom and Megan run in from stage left. Dad and Cooper run in from stage right. They all see Addie at the same time.

ALL: We found her!

MOM: *(bends down to wake up Addie)* Addie! We've been looking all over for you!

DAD: *(relieved but upset)* You know it's against the rules to run away, young lady!

ADDIE: But I didn't run away! You all went to get gifts and left me. So I came to find baby Jesus. His family said they didn't mind if I stayed here until you found me.

Family realizes that they did leave her. All look ashamed. Mom picks up Addie.

ADDIE: Mommy, what is Christmas really about?

MOM: *(all family steps in closer)* It's about the greatest gifts of all—and not what we can buy at a store.

DAD: That's right. It's about celebrating the birth of a Savior and spending time with family. *(pauses)* Let's go home. We don't need to buy more gifts. You all are my greatest gift!

Family turns to walk away. Addie looks back and waves at the manger.

ADDIE: Bye, baby Jesus!

Lights fade.

We Three Kings

by Kayleen Reusser

SUMMARY: *By learning the other verses of this carol, adults will appreciate the importance and symbolism of the gifts given to baby Jesus by the wise men.*

CHARACTERS:
Narrator
Soloist or Choir
Three Wise Men
Joseph
Mary

DIRECTOR'S NOTE: *The three men may appear to be kings with crowns.*

SETTING: *stable where Jesus was born*

PROPS: *baby doll as Jesus, three ornamental containers (like perfume might come in)*

COSTUMES: *fine Middle Eastern biblical apparel for three men; rough, coarse clothing for Joseph and Mary*

Joseph and Mary sit quietly in stable setting on one side of stage. Three Wise Men enter opposite side and stand still. Choir offstage.

CHOIR/SOLOIST: We three kings of Orient are;
   Bearing gifts we traverse afar,
   Field and fountain, moor and mountain,
   Following yonder star.
   O Star of wonder, star of night,
   Star of royal beauty bright,
   Westward leading, still proceeding,
   Guide us to thy perfect light.

NARRATOR: Do you know the definition of a carol? One dictionary says the word *carol* is an Olde English word that refers to "a joyful hymn or religious song, especially one celebrating the birth of Christ." This is the traditional definition of a carol as most of us know it. Christmas carols are like good friends with whom we've grown up. Their words are familiar, and they get us excited about the idea of spending time with family and friends at this special occasion called Christmas. But how many of us really think about the words or know the complete lyrics to our beloved carols? A careful examination of the verses in this carol may offer insights to the significance of Jesus' birth. Let's look at them individually.

CHOIR/SOLOIST: Born a King on Bethlehem's plain,
   Gold I bring to crown Him again,
   King forever, ceasing never,
   Over us all to reign.
   O star of wonder, star of night,
   Star with royal beauty bright,
   Westward leading, still proceeding,
   Guide us to thy perfect light.

NARRATOR: When John Henry Hopkins Jr. penned "We Three Kings" in 1857, he was an Episcopalian deacon from New York City. He focused the song's lyrics and music on the gifts brought to baby Jesus and the gift bearers. He went so far as to name the tune after the men thought by their peers to have been blessed with such considerable insight and knowledge that they were called "wise men." Those men were on a mission. The gospel writer Matthew recorded in his second chapter: "Now after Jesus was born in Bethlehem of Judea in the days of Herod the king, behold, wise men from the East came to Jerusalem, saying, 'Where is He who has been born King of the Jews? For we have seen His star in the East and have come to worship Him.'" (NKJV)

Three Wise Men approach the stable and kneel in front of the baby. Hold out arms filled with containers to baby.

CHOIR/SOLOIST: Frankincense to offer have I;
    Incense owns a Deity nigh;
    Prayer and praising, all men raising,
    Worshiping God on high.
    O Star of wonder, star of night,
    Star with royal beauty bright,
    Westward leading, still proceeding,
    Guide us to thy perfect light.

NARRATOR: "And when they had come into the house, they saw the young Child with Mary His mother, and fell down and worshiped Him. And when they had opened their treasures, they presented gifts to Him: gold, frankincense, and myrrh." Matthew 2: 11 (NKJV).

Sometimes we like to package the story of Jesus' birth, but some things we've been taught are not necessarily true. The Bible does not tell us how many kings there were. Three gifts are mentioned in Matthew's telling of the story, so we assume three men presented them. The gifts were given with godly intent.

Spotlight on two Wise Men who take turns holding their gifts higher than others.

Gold represented Jesus' position as the King of heaven and Earth. Frankincense was thought to be an appropriate gift as a burnt offering to God. The third gift, however, must have seemed sobering, even inappropriate, to offer a newborn baby.

Spotlight on third Wise Man and his gift.

CHOIR/SOLOIST: Myrrh is mine; its bitter perfume
Breathes of life of gathering gloom;
Sorrowing, sighing, bleeding, dying,
Sealed in the stone cold tomb.
O star of wonder, star of night,
Star with royal beauty bright,
Westward leading, still proceeding,
Guide us to thy perfect light.

NARRATOR: Myrrh was commonly used as a burial salve. Its presence reminded people of death. Sad as it must have seemed, myrrh fit baby Jesus' purpose on Earth, as He was sent to give His life to become our sacrifice to God.

CHOIR/SOLOIST: Glorious now behold him arise;
King and God and sacrifice;
Alleluia, Alleluia
Sounds through the earth and skies.
O Star of wonder, star of night,
Star with royal beauty bright,
Westward leading, still proceeding
Guide us to thy perfect light.*

NARRATOR: The wise men's visit and presentation of gifts were sincere and honest expressions of worship. The One whose birth and purpose they had studied for many years and whom they had traveled so far to see was born! They had found Him and could worship Him! Can you picture their excitement?

Wouldn't it be great if our gifts to God, loved ones, and even strangers reflected that same enthusiasm and significance at the season of Jesus' birth? That amount of energy and thought may seem overwhelming, requiring more than we can muster at this busy time of year. I encourage you to at least consider all of the verses to this beautiful carol and be grateful for the three gifts of the wise men. They remind us that Jesus was not only worthy of being presented rare and wonderful gifts but that He also gave us something by coming to Earth: the gift of life eternal.

Lights out.

---

* John Henry Hopkins Jr., "We Three Kings," 1857.

Contributing Authors

DIANA C. DERRINGER

Diana C. Derringer is a writer and blogger. Her work appears in more than thirty-five publications for children, youth, families, and seniors. These include *Clubhouse, Pockets, devozine, ENCOUNTER, Open Windows, The Upper Room, Country Extra, ParentLife, Missions Mosaic, The Christian Communicator*, and *Mature Living*. She also writes radio drama for Christ to the World Ministries. Devotions, drama, practical living, and lessons from life, poetry, and more find a home in her portfolio. Her drama collection, *Beyond Bethlehem and Calvary*, will be released in late 2015. She belongs to the American Christian Writers and the Kentucky State Poetry Society. Visit her at www.dianaderringer.com.

DIANNE GARVIS

Dianne Garvis is a recording artist, vocalist, author, and powerful motivational speaker. Her popular seminar, "Keys to Achieving Excellence," is the culmination of over twenty-five years of business experience in resort management and women's seminars. She's also the founder of The Good Neighbor Program, Inc., a community outreach program for neighbors in need.

Dianne is a graduate of Faith Christian University with a BA in Bible and Theology. She married the love of her life in 1994, and they are blessed with two miracle children.

KAYLEEN REUSSER

Kayleen Reusser has written twelve non-fiction children's books, magazine and newspaper articles, and several *Chicken Soup* stories. As a middle school librarian, she enjoys seeing a student's face light up with the appreciation of a good book. She has self-published a book of World War II stories and is a co-founder of two Christian writing groups. Kayleen speaks regularly to children and adults throughout the US on the importance of reading and writing. Learn more at www.KayleenR.com.

ALICE SULLIVAN

Alice Sullivan has worked in the book publishing industry since 2001 as a ghostwriter, author, writing coach, speaker, and editor. She has worked on over one thousand books, including eleven *New York Times* bestsellers. Some of her more notable clients include Dave Ramsey, Michael Hyatt, Bill Cosby, Thomas Steinbeck, Lee Greenwood, George Foreman III, Pam Tillis, and Judge Andrew Napolitano. She works with publishers, agents, and authors to develop books that are both entertaining and memorable. Visit her at www.alicesullivan.com.

ROB BRITT

Rob was raised the son of a Baptist minister, and his conversion at nine years of age seemed like the natural end to the journey, but it was just the beginning. It began in earnest twenty years later in Dunwoody Baptist Church in Atlanta, Georgia. Early on, he began to work in the church drama department and found his true calling. He helped organize both youth and children's drama ministry teams and is still leading in the children's ministry fourteen years later. He understands what God wants kids to hear and knows God blessed him with the talent to share that knowledge.

SHAYNA DUPRÉ

After falling in love with acting in high school, Shayna knew she had a passion for bringing the stage to life. She began writing sketches and coaching students at her church in Orlando, Florida, for its Fine Arts Competition. Her first year, she and her co-writers won the state title, and Shayna continued competing and winning at the state level for multiple years. In 2008, she entered the college-age national competition and won first place in both the Sketch Writing and Poetry categories. Although she placed in the top ten nationally on several occasions, her piece won first place at the national level in the Large Drama category in 2009.

Ten Questions for Planning Your Best Christmas Programs

1. Who is the audience?

2. How can you approach this Christmas in a fresh way?

3. Will you need special features, including video, dance, music, and staging?

4. Will you want the audience to participate?

5. How long is the service?

6. Will you do one service for kids, youth, and adults?

7. Have times been set for services?

8. Will you need extra seating during the service?

9. What is your budget?

10. Do you need extra volunteers?

Church Survey

Thank you for using this Christmas program book. We would like to know what you think of the dramas. Please send us an email with your comments and thoughts on how we might serve you better.

Paul Shepherd, Shepherd Publishing Services
paul@shepherdps.com

1. What did you think of the program book?

   Excellent   Average   Below Average

2. Which of the following would you like to see more of in future books?

   Dramas   Poems   Stories   Songs

3. Please tell us why you bought the book:

4. What other improvements would you like to see?

5. Would you use an Easter program book?

6. Would you use a year-round program book?

7. Which program book did you use?

   Kids   Youth   Adults

8. If you know of an author who would be interested in contributing to our books, please provide us their name and contact information:

9. Please share the name of your church, primary contact name, phone number, and email address: